ALAN RANGER

15 cm sIG 33
schweres Infanteriegeschütz 33

Published in Poland in 2020
by Wydawnictwo Stratus sp.j.
Po. Box 123,
27-600 Sandomierz 1, Poland
e-mail: office@wydawnictwostratus.pl

as
MMPBooks
e-mail: office@mmpbooks.biz

© Wydawnictwo Stratus sp.j.
© 2020 MMPBooks
© Alan Ranger

www.mmpbooks.biz
www.wydawnictwostratus.pl

ISBN
978-83-65958-98-3

Editor in chief
Roger Wallsgrove

Editorial Team
Bartłomiej Belcarz
Robert Pęczkowski
Artur Juszczak

Cover concept
Dariusz Grzywacz

Book layout concept
Dariusz Grzywacz

All photos: author's collection except stated

DTP
Wydawnictwo Stratus sp.j.

PRINTED IN POLAND

Foreword

In this series of books, I have no intention of trying to add to what is already a very well documented history of Germany's field artillery, as it has been covered by many previous publications. Here I hope to give an impression, through original photographs from my collection taken both during and before war, of the sIG 33 (Heavy Infantry Gun model 1933) and their crews, as they dealt with the conditions and circumstances they found themselves in wherever they served.

In this publication we show what was seen through the lens of the normal German soldier's camera, the soldiers that had to live with and operate these weapons each and every day. Not the professional PK cameramen whose well posed and sanitized shots are well known and have been published over and over again, and as such they have been seen by most interested parties by now already. However the images taken by individual soldiers show a more personal view of the weapons that the soldiers both lived by and worked with, the views that interested the common soldier not the professional propagandist.

For the most part these photographs have been in private collections and have only recently come onto the market. Most of the images we have used here were taken from prints made on old German Agfa paper stock and the majority of these original prints are no more than 25 mm by 45 mm in size. Whilst we have used the best quality photos from my collection, occasionally due to the interesting or the rare nature of the subject matter a photo of a lesser quality has been included.

Introduction

I feel that the first statement that should be made in this short history of the German sIG 33 *schweres Infanteriegeschütz 33*" (Heavy Infantry Gun model 33) is that it was, and still is, the heaviest weapon to ever be classified as an infantry weapon and indeed to be issued to infantry units and to see service with them. The sIG 33 saw service with the German army's infantry throughout the Second World War and was used by them in every theatre of operation in which they fought.

The sIG 33 started its development in 1927, with Rheinmetall-Borsig AG having the final design approved for production in 1933. However due to Germany's deep financial depression of that time, coupled with Rheinmetall's other priorities, the sIG 33 did not enter production until 1936. It was maintained in production until the very end of the war in 1945, with AEG-Fabriken and Böhmische Waffenfabrik AG subcontracted to produce the weapon as well from 1939 onward, to try and keep up with the military's every increasing demands.

With its large 150 mm calibre, the sIG 33 required a substantial gun carriage and recoil system, that combined to produce a very heavy weapon not easily suited to manhandling by the infantry. Its battlefield mobility was always restricted by its service weight of 1,800 kilograms (4,000 pounds), however this weight issue was largely addressed by a change made to the steel used in its production in early 1939. Lighter alloys were used in the gun carriage manufacture and in conjunction with this the gun carriage was redesigned. However production reverted back to the original steel gun carriage in September 1939, with the onset of war requiring the ramping up of aircraft production that had a priority call on all light alloys. This also put an end to the redesigned gun carriage's production, despite the design's completion, thus only a few hundred of the lighter 1,650 kg (3,670 pound) sIG 33/1s were ever produced out of the total production figure of around 4,600 guns.

Whist the original design of the sIG 33 was intended only for towing by horse or other beast of burden, by the late 1930s the German Army was under a motorization plan. Production of the sIG 33 was altered to include in its design pneumatic brakes, that could also be cable operated for when the gun parked up. The motorized design format also called for the addition of vulcanized rubber tyres fitted to the wheel rims in place of the earlier steel bands on the horse drawn type of wheels. As can be seen in this publication, the wheels came in a number of different design formats, from wooden spokes to a variety of pressed steel designs. This was mainly due to the wheels being manufactured by a variety of subcontractors throughout the gun's production life. It should be noted, however, that as the gun carriage design was never changed in production, the sIG 33 never had a sprung suspension fitted to the gun carriage, and so even when towed by a motor vehicle it was not advisable to tow it at more than 16 km/h (10 mph). The weapon system only had the benefit of solid rubber tyres to cushion out any bumps and potholes it might encounter.

The gun carriage also came with a gun recoil spade, that when fitted to the end of the gun carriage's trail prevented the weapon's recoil from moving the gun back too far as it dug into the ground like an anchor. When not in use and the gun was on the move, the gun spade fitted into brackets on top of the gun carriages box structure trail. The sIG 33 was issued with the Rblf36 indirect gunnery sighting optic manufactured by Carl Zeiss AG that was also fitted to a number of other German field pieces,

A trained gun crew was capable of firing three rounds-per-minute. With the sIG 33's muzzle velocity of 790 feet per second it had an effective range of 5,100 yards (4,700 meters). A number of standard types of artillery rounds were available to the sIG 33 that included the I Gr 33, I Gr 38 Nb and the I Gr HI/A

Shell	Type	Weight	Filler
I Gr 33	HE	38 kg (84 lb)	8.3 kg (18 lb) amatol
I Gr 38 Nb	Smoke	40 kg (88 lb)	oleum/pumice
I Gr 39 Hl/A	Hollow-charge	25.5 kg (56 lb)	cyclonite/TNT

The sIG 33 also had an additional type of round made available towards the end of 1942, the *Stielgranate* 42. It was not in common usage and evidence of it in use is hard to find, but it did indeed see service. The *Stielgranate* 42 was different from usual ammunition as it had a driving rod that was loaded into the muzzle end of the barrel that was fixed to the base of a finned projectile much larger than the caliber of the barrel itself, and remained outside the gun tube. A special propellant charge was loaded in the conventional way via the breech that would, when fired, send the projectile 1,000 meters (1,100 yards). The driving rod would fall away from the projectile at around 150 meters (160 yards).

Unlike all other forms of *Stielgranate* made for other weapons, this one was not intended for anti-tank use. It was specifically designed for the demolition of buildings and strongpoints, it was also very good at clearing barbed-wire and minefields by its blast effect alone.

Shell	Type	Weight	Filler
Stielgranate 42	Demolition	90 kg (200 lb)	27 kg (60 lb) amatol

In conclusion, despite the weapon's cumbersome form and excessive weight it proved to be a very valuable and appreciated weapon by the infantry units that were equipped with it. Its value is emphasised by the number of motorised mounts adapted to carry it, such as the *Panzerkampfwagen* I Ausf B (the Bison), the *Panzerkampfwagen* II (also known as Bison), *Panzerkampfwagen* III in two forms, one based on damaged *Panzerkampfwagen* III battle tanks in the field utilizing the superstructure and siG33 guns recovered from mechanically failed *Panzerkampfwagen* II variants, and the second was a standard *Panzerkampfwagen* III hull with a box type superstructure added that was fully enclosed mounting the sIG 33. Lastly two versions were built on the PzKpfw 38(t) chassis as well. They had very different top works but both were called Grille, one was the Sd.Kfz. 138/1 Ausf H (rear engined) the other the Sd.Kfz. 138/1 Ausf M (mid-engined).

This later version of the *schweres Infanteriegeschütz* 33 (sIG 33), that was designed for towing by motorized units, is seen outside its garage in the artillery barracks that was part of the large military complex in Koblenz, Germany. The gun is in overall Panzer grey and has its full set of tools, barrel cleaning rods and sights attached. Note the sighting hatch for direct line-of-sight engagements is open in the gun shield.

Horse drawn type

Here we have a sIG 33 and 18/40 limber combination that is making its way along dirt road somewhere in Russia. A note of irony in the soldiers' humour is seen here as a member of the crew has placed a motor vehicle's number plate on the gun shield of this horse-drawn unit. It was probably designated as a motorized unit but has not as yet received an allocation of vehicles, as was not uncommon in the German army throughout the war.

A very good quality portrait of a gun crew preparing to fire. Of interest is the soldier holding a propellant charge (a brass or steel canister) under his right arm and the soldier holding the actual projectile, an I Gr 33 (HE) high explosive round, whilst he rests it on the gun's trail. The shell is painted light tan and the fuse head is unpainted polished steel. Note in the early part of the war the propellant charge cases were manufactured from brass, but later in the war as brass was becoming scarce, steel was used instead.

A nice study of a *schweres Infanteriegeschütz 33* (sIG 33) in its fully elevated position, this was beyond 45° so that the projectile could be lobbed into a target from above rather than fire on a flatter trajectory into its front. Note the small wooden pole on the ground in front of the main wheel with the leather pad on one end this was used to push the shell fully into the gun's breach when required. Note also the muzzle cap dangling from a cord from the front of the gun, and also the firing lanyard connected to the firing lever on the breech.

This sIG 33 heavy infantry howitzer is being prepared for a fire mission. We can see it has not fired as yet as the gun spade has not yet dug itself into the soft dirt. Note the soldier on the far right of the photograph is holding the firing lanyard that is in turn attached to the gun's shield but not as yet to the gun's trigger.

Bottom: Seen on an icy cold day, this sIG 33 attached to its associated type 18/40 gun limber is being towed by a team of six horses harnessed together through a civilian built up area in the winter of 1939/40. It is unusual to see three of the horses being ridden at once but not unique; it was far more common to see just the lead horse being ridden. Note the set of equipment carried on the gun shield is missing the spade.

Passing through a Belgian town in May 1940, this horse-drawn artillery unit will find it hard to keep up with the speed of the rest of the advance. For example, the majority of the artillery that laid down fire on to the Dunkirk beaches took another day to get into position, such was the speed of the motorized advance.

This photo was taken in the artillery barracks at Meppen, Germany, on 23rd April 1939, only days before the unit was part of the invasion forces that took part in *Fall Rot* (Case Red), the invasion of France and the attack on the BEF (British Expeditionary Force).

This photograph illustrates to good advantage the sIG 33 being used in the direct fire role. Note the gunner with his eye pressed against the gun sight looking through the open sighting hatch in the gun shield. Of note is that the gun's cleaning poles are missing, one can assume that they have been used and are at the ready somewhere close to the gun position.

In this photo we can see the indirect fire sights and the sight extension tube that could be used to extend the sight height above the gun shield. As we can see here the sighting hatch is closed. Of note is the large white letter "A" painted on the inner side of the gun shield - this tells us that this is gun A in what was usually a four-gun battery (A, B, C & D).

Taken from under the portico of this commandeered French chateaux, being used as the HQ of an infantry unit that is part of the garrison forces maintained in France following the capitulation. We see a pair of sIG 33s that are being used as ceremonial guards either side of a dais/ lectern that is being used by the unit's CO to address his troops.

Making their way down another mud road we see this six horse team towing an 18/40 gun limber attached to a sIG 33 heavy infantry howitzer. Of note is the bale of hay, to be used as fodder for the horses, slung over the gun.

This gun crew portrait was taken in Bielefeld, Germany, in the summer of 1938. Note the NCO standing next to the officer holding the two part cleaning pole that has been screwed together and has one of the cleaning tools attached, a copper wire brush in this case. Also note the I Gr 33 (HE) high explosive round set on top of a brass propellant cartridge in the foreground, the shell itself would not have stood upright on its own as its base was not flat, so it has been set on the propellant cartridge case to hold it upright.

Bottom: Also taken at the artillery barracks in Bielefeld, this photo was taken on July 4th 1937 and shows a brand new sIG 33 in the pre-war three tone camouflage of green, yellow/tan and brown that has just been received by this unit. The weapon it replaced in the unit, that is seen in the background on its purpose-made trailer, is a German heavy trench mortar, a relic from the First World War that was phased out completely before the end of 1938.

Here we see the results of a burst barrel; it has blown both the main part of the barrel off and also completely destroyed the recoil system. However unlike many other weapons, the sIG 33 was so robustly constructed that damaged gun would most likely have been sent back for a rebuild. Lastly of note here are the guns markings painted in white on the inner side of the gun shield – "D2", the D denotes that this is the 4th gun in its battery and the "2" denotes that it is a gun from the 2nd battery in the artillery unit.

Bottom: This unit has been assembled for a promotion ceremony on 17th July 1940. Of interest is that all the assembled equipment, the PzKpfw I (*Panzerkampfwagen* I) Ausf Bs and the 37 mm Pak 36/37 anti-tank guns as well as the mounts for the machine guns, are in Panzer Grey but the two sIG 33s are still in their pre-war three tone camouflage scheme.

Photographed whilst awaiting orders in the midst of the rubble of a shelled-out part of the French village of Hirson, where only days before the German vanguard had run into a French defensive line. We have a sIG 33 in full travel mode, the gun trail spade is in its brackets on top of the gun's trail and the leather barrel end protective cap is in place.

This action shot was taken in November 1941 on the central Russian front, the gun crew still in their summer uniforms must be feeling the cold. Note in contrast the NCO in the background, with binoculars around his neck, wearing a greatcoat and a woollen scarf wrapped around his face.

This relaxed-looking group are actually setting up to fire on the beaches of the Dunkirk pocket in late May 1940. This sIG 33 has been dug in on the reverse slope of a bank for protection from any possible return fire.

Bottom: A gun crew on the coast of the Baltic Sea are undertaking a spot of firing practice during their training. Note the NCO holding what is probably the gun's firing record log book. The ammunition can clearly be seen with a corporal holding an I Gr 33 shell, another soldier holding the propellant charge cartridge is at the far end of the line of troops on the far side of the gun.

Another photo taken during training on the use and maintenance of the sIG 33. The gun has its sight extension tube fitted to the gun sight to enable it to see over the gun shield. The training is being carried out in barracks and as such none of the field equipment has been issued or installed.

A four gun battery is seen here parked on the assembly yard of the gun firing range located in the military training grounds on Luneburg Heath in northern Germany. Note the two guns closest have had the recoil spades unhitched and the two in the rear still have them stowed on their trails.

This scene is from an open day at the barracks. A local child is playing soldier with the crew of this gun. The German Army held many such events during the National Socialist time frame as it was part of the Nazi doctrine that the army was the state and the people were the army. All were one in the Greater German Reich. Sadly such propaganda worked and led the German nation into a war they would ultimately lose.

This sIG 33 is being set up as part of an exhibition in a German town's park for the public to view. Note the pre-war camouflage scheme on this gun, the three tonal values are easily to see and clearly defined. They are RAL-8010 Brown, RAL-6007 Green and RAL-8002 Earth Yellow (Tan Yellow).

On the perimeter of the final phases of the battle towards the entrapment of the BEF on the Dunkirk beaches, this photo was taken on the outskirts of Ostend, Belgium. Of interest, other than the calm demeanour of the gun crew, is the French helmet attached to the gun shield, a souvenir of their campaign to date and the barrel cap slung on the end of the recoil slide.

Bottom: A gun crew prepare to fire their sIG 33. The lanyard to the trigger is held firm ready to pull to fire the gun. Note the wood tamping tool lent up against the wheel, it is part of the gun's equipment and was used for either knocking out a jammed cartridge case should one get stuck in the breech or pushing a shell into the breach when required. These tools are made of wood so that they would not produce a spark when used, just in case any undetonated explosive remained in the barrel.

Here we have a battery of sIG 33s firing from a well camouflaged position on the reverse slope of a hill in northern France in the 1940 invasion. Note the NCO with his firing log book - he will note the shot fall and the settings on the gun to achieve them, and then will use the firing table to bring the shots onto target. The gun seen here is laying down indirect fire by lobbing shells up and over whatever protection the enemy is hidden behind. Lastly, note the gun barrel is seen at full recoil.

An atmospheric photograph of a lone sIG 33 looking from behind as it is about to start a fire mission on the Russian steppe. The enormity of the task to take the vast expanse that is Russia has never been more obvious than in this image.

Mobility was always the sIG 33's main problem and in the freezing Russian winter the horses that had gone east stood little chance of survival in the open. Most sadly perished before the winter of 1941/42 was through. This led to many different expedient solutions being used to move the guns. Here a truck is being used to carry the type 18/40 limber and, although the gun has no suspension whatsoever, it is to be towed by the motor vehicle anyway.

Bottom: Another view of the same scene only seconds later, the limber now loaded and the gun hitched to the towing shackle ready for the off. The gun crew take a moment to pose for the photo.

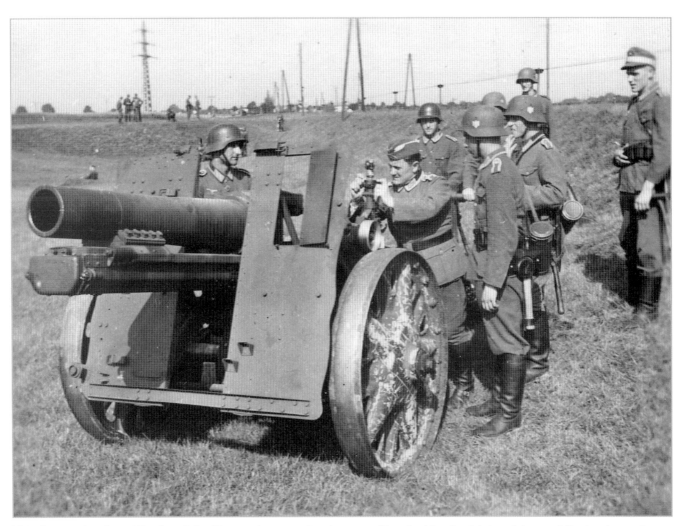

This photograph, taken whilst the unit is taking part in an exercise, shows an officer checking the sighting of the gun following the ranging calculations of the crew. In the back ground one of the exercise's umpires, with the white band around his cap, looks on.

Bottom: Seen here a horse-drawn *schweres Infanteriegeschütz 33* (sIG 33) unit is crossing a German temporary, but well-made, wooden bridge crossing the Dnieper river in Russian in August of 1941. Note the two helmets hung over the handle of one of the tools stowed on the front of the gun shield.

This unit is on the move through the hills of eastern Latvia in the autumn of 1941. Of interest are the covers over the gun's breech, sighting equipment and also the folded wicker 'mattress' stowed on the gun's trail, lodged between the stowed trail spade and a cross member of the gun's trail. This would be laid on the ground and ammunition unpacked onto it, to prevent mud getting onto the rounds.

Bottom: A well camouflaged horse-drawn sIG 33 passes a horse-drawn standard large combat infantry wagon type Hf. 7 on 15th September 1941, but sadly I have no location.

Here we have a nice close-up study of a sIG 33 that the crew are busy cleaning. We can see the open tool locker that is an integral part of the gun's trail with its lid open and some of its internal stowage is in evidence. Also seen here is a crew man sitting on a wooden ammunition box that holds six of the propellant charge cartridges and is marked for the sIG 33.

This close-up finds the crew of a sIG 33 taking a drink break with all four of the visible crew members having the cups from the top of their water bottles in hand. The detail in this photo offers us a good view of the two part cleaning poles it is interesting to see the metal end caps with a threaded rod at the very tip, one was used to screw the two halves of the pole together and the other to hold one of the cleaning tools in place.

A fire support mission in Yugoslavia in support of anti-partisan operations in the mountains around Sarajevo in the winter of 1942/43. The sIG 33 is in full recoil with the barrel seen at the very limit of its movement down the recoil slide, the extension tube is also seen fitted to the gun sights.

This horse-drawn artillery unit equipped with sIG 33s is seen advancing towards the Russian town of Berdychiv in the late summer of 1941. Unusual here is the tarpaulin that has been stretched over both the 18/40 limber and the sIG 33 gun, and the way it has been tied down gives a very sloppy appearance to the gun's stowage. The large sack of fodder on the gun's breech does not help the look either

The town of Kiev (Kyiv) lies ravaged on the other of the river Dnieper while on our side a sIG 33 and its team are making their way towards a temporary wooden pontoon bridge. This can be seen in place directly on top of the bridge destroyed in the earlier bombing of the city and even making use of some of the original stone bridge's arch piles.

Seen in the grounds of a farm this sIG 33 is in firing position. Note the rattan shell carrying case on the ground next to the gun. It has a red painted band around it that indicates that it was carrying an I Gr 38 NB Smoke shell.

In its firing position this snow-bound sIG 33 has its sight extension tube fitted yet the direct fire sight hatch is open as well. Other things to note are the firing lanyard attached to the trigger in the breech block held taut and the barrel's protective cap hanging from its retaining strap attached to the top of the barrel's recoil slide rail.

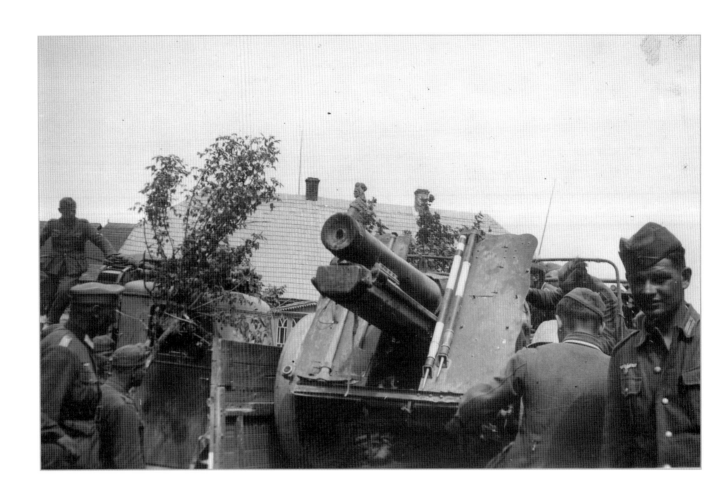

Both the photographs on this page show a horse-drawn unit on the outskirts of Gent, Belgium, during the advance into the West in 1940. They are loading their sIG 33 onto a commandeered lorry in an attempt to try and keep up with the speed of the motorized vanguard of the advance. The lower photograph shows the loaded sIG 33 now being wedged into position to prevent it moving around on the back of the lorry, to prevent damage to both it and the truck it now relies on for movement. No doubt the horses were left behind and would take some time to catch up with the unit until the speed of the advance slowed during the siege of the BEF in the Dunkirk pocket.

In the corner of this field a sIG 33 is being prepared to fire. A senior NCO is checking the gunner's sight settings and as usual the gun's commander is making a note of the setting and type of ammo used for the gun's firing log.

In the snow this type 18/40 limber attached its associated sIG 33 has overturned. This may well be trickier to sort out than it appears, as the axle and wheel hub might very well be damaged.

Bottom: A German artillery position on the reverse slopes of a hill in northern France in 1940. This sIG 33 is awaiting orders and the crew is seen relaxed, one reading a newspaper and others posing for a private photo in a small group by the gun's wheel, with one of them holding an I Gr 33 shell as a prop. Of note is the foliage being used as camouflage, with the 18/40 gun limber being hidden by foliage completely.

Opposite page, top: This sIG 33 in the snow in 1941 is being used as a backdrop for these two soldiers to pose with for photographs to send home. One has his great coat on and a makeshift balaclava, probably made from a blanket, and the other wearing a coat (*Wachtmantel*) issued to sentries. The inscription on the gun barrel says War Christmas Eve 1941.

This photograph proves beyond doubt that one picture is worth a thousand words, as the simple notation on its reverse tells us "Stuck in Russia with all horses now dead". These two sombre-looking crew members stand next to their sIG 33 gun and limber that have become stuck and subsequently frozen into the mud and await their salvation to arrive. In this case of this crew it eventually turned out to be a captured Russian truck.

This interesting photograph is of a sIG 33 being loaded onto a steam freighter in the Italian port of Genoa for shipment on to the North African port of Benghazi, Libya, on its way to become part of the German Africa-Korps in the winter of 1941/42.

Bottom: The crew of this gun are seen struggling to man handle their sIG 33 into its final firing position and whilst the weapons official description was "Heavy Infanterie Gun" it actually referred to the weight of the shot it fired but one can easily see why it is often though that it referred to the weight of the weapon itself. Note how two of the gun crew are using the stamped holes in the steel wheels as leverage points to help roll the gun into position.

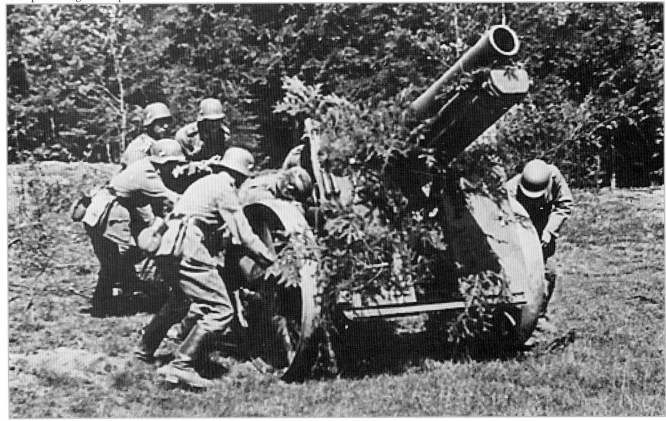

This action photo shows a crew with their hands cupped over their ears to try and protect them from damage caused by the concussive blast effect of firing the gun. The gunner with the trigger lanyard in hand is about give it a tug to fire the weapon. This photo was taken on the firing line formed to lay down a barrage on the BEF pocket confined on the Dunkirk beaches. Written on the photo's reverse a notation states "firing on Loon Plage 1st of June 1940".

Another photo taken of the same gun as above on the same day. Here we can clearly see all the field tools removed, no doubt being used some-where, and the barrel's protective leather cap stowed on the end of the recoil slide. One of the gunners is adjusting the gun's aiming point to the side, he does not need to use the sight as the length of the shot fall has already been set. He is just making a small adjustment to the side to maximise the effect of the barrage and not hit the same spot twice.

This badly creased photo has been included as I feel it offers us a good view of the sIG 33 in an open firing position on a cold day in the winter of 1941/42, none of the gun crew have any winter clothing in evidence other than the two gunners both wearing gloves, the full corporal without gloves is holding his binoculars and that may be why he is not wearing them, lastly none of them are wearing their steel helmets but the gunner seen to be smoking has his strapped onto his belt.

A good portrait of a sIG 33 and it crew setting up the weapon to fire they are being watched by one of their senior officers who is standing in the foreground, of note here is the crew member holding on to the guns lifting "T" bar that is attached to the guns trail spade, the crewman using the gun sights and lastly the gun's commander with his back to us making a note in the gun's firing record log book.

This sIG 33 is positioned in an orchard with branches laid against the wheels as part of the position's camouflage. The crew seems relaxed and the gun is not set up to fire - its barrel's end cap is on, the wet weather cover is over the sighting mechanism and the guns breech. Lastly there is no pile close by of ready ammunition.

Here we have a close-up of a sIG 33. In the foreground we see the top of the lifting handle that was installed in the end of the gun's trail or in the gun's trail spade to enable the gun to be manoeuvred by hand within its firing position. Also seen are the top edges of two rattan shell carrying tubes. The gunner on the extreme right of the photo has his hand on the opening lever for the breech block, and it is seen in the fully open position.

Taken as a gun troop are preparing for a visit/inspection whilst in the field from a high ranking official, this group of soldiers are seen in full uniform in parade condition, a situation that would never be seen had the official not been on the way. I can assure you from personal experience, in the field you wear/carry whatever you need or feel comfortable in, and the first thing to be taken off when not needed is your helmet. Of note on the sIG 33 itself is that, whilst the cleaning poles are in their correct stowed position, the other field tools such as the spade and pick-axe are missing.

A photograph of another inspection taking place, this time on a training ground attached to a barracks complex. Whilst the officer pats the gun barrel knowingly, his aide-de-camp and NCO is seen wearing a map case that was also often used to hold orders and/or a note pad.

A clear shot showing a gun being pulled at walking pace, with officers following on horseback. Another officer is walking beside the gun, demonstrating the very slow speed of movement of these guns.

An informative picture here of this sIG 33 is being prepared to fire. The soldier on the far right is untangling the firing lanyard before attaching one end to the gun's trigger, located on the right-hand side of the breech block. Another is getting the sighting optic out of its fitted container within the tool box in the gun's trail. Also of note is the fitted gun's trail spade and the manoeuvring handlebars also in position, fitted into their mounting on the trail spade.

This badly creased photograph has been included as it still offers us a very good view of a sIG 33 and its crew seated in parade formation from close up. Mostly this view is only photographed from a distance and detail is lacking. Here we can see the towing rig in some detail that I hope both researchers and modellers will find of use.

Hidden behind a small hedge this sIG 33 seen in central Russia in the winter of 1941/42. The photo was actually taken on 3rd February 1942. The gun has had a coat of whitewash over its Panzer grey paint, that is now beginning to wear off with both rain and handling, giving an interesting finish to the gun. Note the two crew members on the right preparing a shell with its fuse ready to be fired.

A four-horse team tows this sIG 33 behind the standard heavy infantry howitzer limber type 18/40. The limber weighed 0.617 tons, it was a robust unit but possibly overweight from the start, even before it was loaded up with supplies.

This photo of an infantry unit's heavy support group equipped with sIG 33s was taken during a parade on route through the city centre of Dortmund, Germany, as part of the city's celebrations for Hitler's birthday in April 1938.

This photo is of a horse-drawn sIG 33 and its associated troops, as seen in the field. A notable contrast to the parade photo seen earlier in this publication! Note the more relaxed dress of the troops and the tarpaulin slung over the shield and gun carriage of the weapon, also the metal pail/bucket being held in place by being slung on the retaining strap for the gun barrel's protective cap.

On a firing range in late 1939 we see a sIG 33 in full recoil having just been fired. Note in the background we see a neat gathering of rattan shell protective tubes and the gun crew's rifles stood in threes

A fine close-up of the rear trail of a sIG 33. In the foreground of the photo on top of the back portion of the trail we see the manoeuvring bar mounting pointing and its associated locking handle. In this photo the spade is fitted and the manoeuvring bar is fitted to the mounting point on that, and can be just be seen on very far left of the photo.

This view of a gunner sitting on a sIG 33 gun's trail writing a letter home was taken outside the Belgian town of Aalst on the evening of 18th May 1940. Note the heavily loaded 18/40 gun limber and the trail spade stowed in its travel position.

Another horse-drawn sIG 33 is seen here pre-war on manoeuvres within the training area on Luneburg Heath. Of note is the kit stowed on the saddle of the horse closest to the camera and view offered by the photo of the tack on the horses in full towing configuration. The white letter "A" on the inside of the gun shield tells us that the gun is the first gun in its battery of four guns.

Making its way through the Ardennes as part of the invasion force in the battle for the west, this horse-drawn sIG 33 and crew struggle to get their weapon up this hill. Its six horse team pull this sIG 33 and type 18/40 gun limber whilst the crew push. It was all part of the plan that the armoured division would use the few available metalled roads whilst secondary units would make their way along other routes, such as forest tracks and dirt roads.

This sIG 33 is set up in a firing position in the south of a battle in the Ukraine. It is a Russian solder we see featured in this photograph, judging by his helmet and coat. Captured Russians were often treated badly, and his happy expression suggests that he may be a Hiwi (*Hilfswilliger* – volunteer helper) working for the Germans.

Here we see loaded onto Deutsche-Reichsbahn railway flatbeds the heavy weapons troop from an infantry regiment. This photo was taken in September 1941 at the marshalling yards of Leipzig station and the train is on its way to the occupied Polish city of Lviv (today in Ukraine), where there was a major station yard were trains would have to change their loads from wagons made to run on the European gauge to wagons that would run on the (wider) Russian gauge.

This sIG 33 is emplaced and is being readied to commence fire as part of a prepared bombardment fire order, no doubt as a prelude to an attack somewhere on the front. The gun was camouflaged by the trees that were piled over it that have now been moved away. The ready pile of ammunition is still partially covered but some of the rattan shell protective tubes can be seen under the cover that is in the process of being removed by one of the crew. Lastly of note is the white letter "B" that denotes that the gun is the second gun in the battery of four.

Motorised towing type

Here we see a motorized version of the sIG 33, easily identified as such by the vulcanized solid rubber tyres on the pressed steel wheels. The crew are sighting the gun in on a target and the gun captain, normally an NCO, is noting the sight settings in the weapon's fire log. I doubt that the tree branches lent up against the gun's shield and recoil system will remain there following the blast effect of the first round fired.

This beautiful profile study is of a sIG 33 of the type intended for towing by a motorized vehicle. The clarity of this photo allows us to see the stencilled lettering in white on the recoil slide, that reads "braun". It indicates that the recoil system has been filled with braun hydraulic fluid as opposed to the ark hydraulic fluid that was formulated for icy conditions. The two fluids were from quite early on mixed together and this was usually seen noted on recoil systems as "braun/ark". This mix of hydraulic fluids became the standard in the latter part of the war.

The crew in this photograph look quite relaxed in the cold, in not much else but there normal field uniform. I can only assume that there is no wind, as the wind chill factor on days such as this would be punishing in only these uniforms. This sIG 33 that has been emplaced in a small dug-out has been painted with whitewash over its standard Panzer Grey paint job. It is notable that in many areas the whitewash has started to wear off.

The next few shots come from an album that belonged to a *Gefreiten* (Corporal) Max Gleb, who served with the *257. Infanterie-Division* wich was part of *Heeresgruppe Süd* (Army Group South) during the invasion of Poland in September 1939.

This one of the very early sIG 33s to be fitted with vulcanized rubber tyres for motorized towing. However it has hit a mine buried in the verge of this Belgian road by the retreating BEF or Belgian army, south of the port town of Ostend. It has blown off one of the main wheels and caused the gun to roll over. The integral tool box in the gun's trail has nearly lost its lid and the main elevation hand wheel has also come away and is seen in the foreground. This gun would have been returned to Germany but was probably scrapped, as the frame likely buckled and it would not have been cost effective to repair it.

Here we have sIG 33 gun also from the *Artillerie-Regiment 257*, but seen here in a well-prepared firing position both dug in and camouflaged by felled small fir trees in a wooded area north west of Kraków, Poland. Of note is the small "MAX" painted in white on the barrel.

Again we see the *Artillerie-Regiment 257*, here in a railway yard cleaning their sIG 33s after unloading them from the long train journey. The crew are seen here fitting one of the two cleaning tools to the other cleaning rod. The tool that is seen being screwed onto the cleaning rod in the lower photo is a round leather padded bag that is the same size as the guns bore and has cotton wadding wrapped around it to clean carbon residue from the barrel. The other tool was more aggressive as it was a copper wire brush head that would be used to clean the residue from the rifling grooves. Once used the wire brush made a real mess in the barrel and the other tool would be needed to clean the mess out and then fine clean and polish the bore using many wraps of cotton wadding.

This photo, although not the best quality, is of interest as shows quite clearly the sIG 33 in firing condition, sights fitted and the barrel end cap removed but hanging from its retaining strap. Lastly note the lifting bar, here attached to the gun's trail spade on the far right of the photo.

A badly damaged sIG 33 photographed in Russia in the winter of 1942/43. Note the missing side of the gun shield and the broken end cap to the recoil slide. Half of it has fallen off and the gun barrel has slid partially down the recoil slide.

This sIG 33 was photographed on a Baltic coast firing range and gives us a great view of the gun recoil slide and the firing lanyard attached to the gun's trigger, located on the breech block. We can also see clearly in this view the aperture in the gun shield left when the sighting hatch is open.

A parade in Leipzig in the summer of 1941. We see the heavy weapon infantry support unit of an infantry division equipped with the *schweres Infanteriegeschütz 33* (sIG 33), the heaviest weapon issued to any infantry unit of any of the combatants during the war. The guns are being towed by Sd.Kfz. 10 Ausf As.

Both the photographs on the top of this page were taken in the winter of 1943/43 and are of the same freshly whitewashed sIG 33. Note on the picture on the right the solder wearing the straw over-boots. Copied from Russian examples, "*strohschuhe*" were relatively commonly issued during the middle part of WW2 in the extremes of winter. The German troops in general had learned the lessons of the previous winter and most had far better winter clothing.

Bottom: The sIG 33 in this photograph is hidden in a well-camouflaged gun firing position. The crew can be seen cleaning the barrel as part of the preparation for a fire mission latter in the day.

This sIG 33 is seen being prepared to fire. One gunner has the gun's breech fully open and another is running the gun through its traversing radius to ensure smooth operation during the fire mission, his right hand firmly gripping the turning wheel's handle. The sIG 33 was able to be traversed by 11.5° to either side of the centre line. Lastly the gun is seen to still have a cover over the rear part of the barrel, on the far side of the gun shield.

This atmospheric photograph was taken in late October 1941 just after the first snows of the coming winter. The sIG 33 is seen in recoil having just fired a round towards the city centre of Leningrad (Saint Petersburg). The gun is still in its Panzer grey finish and the crew are still wearing their standard field uniform. They have tried to camouflage the gun by covering it in a couple of white sheets, but this has had little effect. Note the rattan protective tubes in the foreground, most of which appear to be empty. A gunner to the left of the photo is bent over a pile of full ammunition tubes

Here we see a memorial service parade in progress with sIG 33s set to fire in salute for the German dead. Such services were a feature of the early war years but became virtually non-existent as the war progressed.

In this railyard we find two distinctly different weapons, one a throwback to World War One, the sIG 33 heavy Infantry howitzer, and the other a state of the art weapon for the day, a 75 mm Pak 40 anti-tank gun. Of note fitted on the sIG 33 are the rare wooden spoked wheels with steel rims covered with solid vulcanized rubber tyres. This type of wheel was the least common amongst the many types regularly used on the sIG 33.

Bottom: This group of gunners are squatting close to their sIG 33 and are setting fuse heads for the coming bombardment. In the rear of the photo we can see rounds ready with their fuse caps fitted.

In this Russian homestead a sIG 33 crew are seen placing their weapon in its new firing position. In the background we can see a pile of wooden crates - these hold the propellant charge cartridges, with six cartridges being stowed in each box.

This photo shows Max Gleb (marked with an "X") who served with the *Artillerie-Regiment 257* in the winter of 1941/42. This informal portrait was taken on December 18th on the Russian front. Sadly I have no more photos from that date on.

Taken on 12th January 1943 this sIG 33 was taking part in supporting anti-partisan operations in Yugoslavia. Note two of the gunners have reversible style camouflage jackets, whilst the other two are still in the older pattern uniform, one wearing a greatcoat. The sIG 33 is in a worn whitewash finish but looks to be in very good condition overall.

This is a great photograph to give an explanation on how a sIG 33 operates. We see the weapon itself in a firing position, a wooden rod being used to push a shell into the barrel, the gunner in the white shirt holding the breech open, the gunner behind all the others is holding a propellant cartridge and there is a row of ready ammunition in the foreground laid on blankets. The large wooden boxes held six propellant cartridges and we can see a small stack of them have been placed on some of those boxes.

A rare photo of a gun carriage undergoing maintenance. This sIG 33 looks to be having its axle rod
worked on and also the braking system that was
included on this later production example of the gun.
The brake drum can be clearly seen on the wheel
resting against the front of the gun, whist the actual
braking hub is not in view and has been removed
from the gun carriage completely. No doubt it is
being worked on elsewhere. Lastly of note the gun
breech block has also been removed for work to be
carried out, but this was not uncommon and came
under routine maintenance.

This close-up of a gun in firing position is posed for a member of the crew to take a photo for his album and was taken on a range that was part of the military training grounds on Luneburg Heath. The main clue to it being posed is that if the gun was loaded and the gunner pulled that hard on the trigger lanyard the gun would have fired, and the cameraman from where he is standing would now be deaf and probably suffering from concussion.

This photo was taken on 11th June in pasture south-east of Saint Valery, one of the last holdouts of the remnants of the rear-guard that were left in France after they protected the evacuation from Dunkirk. This sIG 33 is about to start firing on the town on this the last day of the battle.

This photo shows two sIG 33s that were damaged by mines. The towing vehicles have been recovered for repair but the sIG 33s will have to await their turn to be recovered, if indeed they are assessed to be recoverable. The rounds from one of the recovered vehicles have been off-loaded and will hopefully be picked up latter. This photograph was taken close to the Belgian town of Kortrijk on 24th May 1940 as the main advance of the Germans closed in on Dunkirk, some 50 miles to the north-west.

Another photograph of the sIG 33 pictured on the bottom of page 51, here we see a group of officers assessing the potential recovery of the gun that, when damaged, sunk into the soft mud that has now frozen solid and trapped the gun in place. Sadly I do not have any photos that tell me the if the gun was eventually recovered or not.

A good photo from the mid war period, it was taken in the summer of 1943 on the Russian front in the grounds of a large house. Of note is that by 1943 more camouflage was required as the *Luftwaffe* no longer could ensure air superiority over battlefield, so such emplacements needed to be hidden better from roaming Russian aircraft.

This sIG 33 is also well hidden in its gun emplacement. Whilst most of the gun crew seem to be relaxing, the soldier in the foreground is preparing a fuse setting for one of the I Gr 33 high explosive shells. Note the small wooden boxes - these are the smaller of the two standard boxes the propellant cartridges were packed into. Only two cartridges could be stowed in this box type, but unlike the larger boxes these were easily handled by one soldier.

This is a good photo of a quickly prepared firing position. The crew have placed branches from a tree next to the gun to aid in its concealment and also rested one branch up against the gun shield itself. A crew member is seen securing it in position, whilst another gunner is adjusting the sights to the target and the last gunner in the photo is adjusting the longitudinal axis of the gun to the position called out by the gunner operating the gun sight. The gun's trail spade has been dug in and the crew's hand spade is stuck in the ground close by. The smaller type of ammunition box, containing only two propellant cartridges, can be seen piled up to the right of the gun. The steel bar seen lying on top of the pile of dirt is one of the two lifting bars supplied with each gun that fitted in brackets, one each side of the gun and under two hook type castings we can clearly see on the gun's trail, close to the ground. They were for the crew to use to move the gun around more easily, as two crew men could lift at each bar and by the applied extra leverage it made the lift relatively easy.

This photo is a nice relaxed portrait of the gun crew, looking quite relaxed even though they are in a firing position close to the French coast. They have been taking part in the bombardment of the remnants of the BEF in the town of Saint-Valery-en-Caux most of that day, 11th June 1940.

On a cold November morning in northern Ukraine this sIG 33 and its crew are photographed whilst about start preparing the gun for a change in position. You can see by the wheel tracks in the snow that the gun has been traversed by nearly 80° to the right, in order to be able to engage its next target. The restricted lateral movement of the gun on its carriage was a disadvantage when a large section of the front needed to be covered or tracking a mobile enemy.

A typical firing position here in the snow just outside a Russian town in the winter of 1941/42. It is common for artillery of any nation to hide its artillery close to or behind buildings for a number of reasons, mainly for the extra cover offered and that it conceals the exact firing position from any enemy observer looking to call in a counter strike against the attacking battery.

This is rather tired photo that is badly water damaged yet still shows an interesting scene. It is a gun and crew in central Russia in May of 1942. We can see the barrel protective end cap hanging from its retaining strap and both the lifting "T" beam attached to the gun's trail spade and also one of the two lifting bars in the lifting position, with one of the crew members standing over its end. It's hard to say who took the photo, as a standard gun crew consisted of eight crew members and all eight are visible in the shot.

Another shot of a sIG 33 being readied for action. The gunner closest to the camera is both looking through the sight and operating the elevation mechanism hand wheel. The trail spade has the "T" beam attached to enable the crew to move the trail when required.

Not a common sight to see on any front was an Sd.Kfz. 251 armoured half-track towing a sIG 33. These valuable vehicles were usually only issued to Panzer Grenadiers and rarely to motorized infantry units but hardly ever, if ever, to a heavy support unit of an infantry regiment. We can assume that the '251' was being used purely as an expedient measure as no other suitable transport was available at the time.

This relaxed looking portrait was taken in the early days of the headlong charge into the vast Russian steppe. At this point in the attack it looked like Hitler had been correct when he stated "All we have to do is kick the door down and the whole rotten edifice will tumble down". In these early days the Russian army fell away in front of Hitler's juggernaut, and these troops were probably as troubled by the all-pervading dust as they were by the Russian troops. That was to change fast as the weather turned.

One of my few late war photos, this was taken in autumn of 1944 on the Western Front somewhere in Holland, but sadly I have no more information on this well-hidden gun position or the crew who are manning it. Unfortunately like most photos I have purchased individually from the internet they have been ripped out of albums and no consideration has been given to recording any caption written in the album. Sometimes you are lucky and there is a notation on the reverse but this is a rarity, not the norm.

This atmospheric photograph taken in Russia in October 1943 shows a Sd.Kfz. 10 Ausf B. Note the tilt is in the raised position as is the driver's windshield. The vehicle is towing a 15 cm sIG 33, well wrapped up to keep it clean on this very muddy cross-country journey.

This posed shot taken on the Munster training grounds gives a nice profile view of a late 1942 production Sd.Kfz. 10 D7 Ausf B towing a 15 cm sIG 33. Note the crew, all in full uniform straight from the barracks. In the field this would never happen as items of uniform get old and worn out or just lost, and personal comfort is a priority, not uniformity. The first thing to be removed would have been their helmets in any non-combat situation.

Stielgranate 42

Opposite page: This is a photo from an ordnance report and the top part of the image is a nice close-up of the war head and stabilizing fins of the *Stielgranate* 42 loaded in the barrel of a sIG 33. The lower part of the photo shows the whole sIG 33 with the *Stielgranate* 42 loaded into the end of the barrel. Note even here in this preliminary ordnance intelligence report the projectile is wrongly denoted as an "A.T. Grenade" (Anti-tank weapon).

This is a cutaway sketch of the *Stielgranate* 42 warhead end, the solid fuel rocket motor pole has been sectioned to fit the page. A common error made in some of the publications I have read is that it was an anti-tank projectile, like so many other of the muzzle-loaded ordnance manufactured to be fired from otherwise obsolete or other purpose weapons such as Flak guns. The German weapons ordnance office produced more of these types of projectiles than any other combatant, but the *Stielgranate* 42 was purely a high explosive projectile built for blast effect for the demolition of buildings and other defensive hard points. It was not available in any other form such as hollow charge for armour penetration.

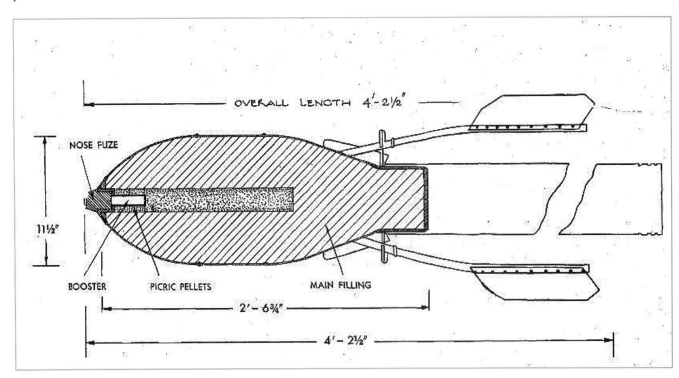

70

15 CM. SIG' 33 AND HEAVY A. T. GRENADE

This photo is of a demonstration of the *Stielgranate* 42 to a unit equipped with the sIG 33. Note the pile of wooden ammunition crates that contain the war head of the *Stielgranate* 42 to the left of the gun in the photo. On top of the pile is a box full of fins yet to be attached.